FADED GLORY

AIRLINE COLOUR SCHEMES OF THE PAST

FADED GLORY

AIRLINE COLOUR SCHEMES OF THE PAST

JOHN K. MORTON

Airlife
England

AUTHOR'S NOTE

John K. Morton started taking photographs of airliners in 1970 and his pictures, reproduced here selected from a collection of 10,000, were all taken on Kodachrome 25 film.

Faded Glory. Airline Colour Schemes of the Past is not intended to be a reference book, but merely a selection of photographs of commercial airliners which cannot now be seen. Many of the airlines shown throughout the book have departed the aviation scene whilst those remaining have since adopted a new colour scheme.

The author hopes this volume of pictures will give the reader as much pleasure and interest as he achieved whilst on location in various parts of the world.

Copyright © 1991 John K. Morton

First published in the UK in 1991 by
Airlife Publishing Limited

British Library Cataloguing in Publication Data
Morton, John
 Faded glory.
 1. Airlines. Liveries
 I. Title
 387.7

 ISBN 1-85310-088-9

Printed in Singapore by Kyodo Printing PTE Ltd.

Airlife Publishing Ltd.

101 Longden Road, Shrewsbury SY3 9EB, England

CONTENTS LIST

BRANIFF

Originally founded by brothers Paul and Tom Braniff, the airline started operations in 1930. Based in Dallas, Texas, the carrier became victim of deregulation and ceased operations in 1982. Services were restarted on a very much reduced scale in 1984 but were again suspended in September 1989 after filing for chapter 11 bankruptcy. Several attempts have since been made to re-commence services, although at press time Braniff is still not airborne again.

Boeing 727 N471BN, one of many Boeing tri-jets flown by the company on its extensive North American routes. Shown in the last style of livery before ceasing operations in 1982 the 727 is at the carrier's home base Dallas/Fort Worth in July 1980.

Left: Services to the Far East and Europe were provided by Braniff, and during the 1970s the airline obtained Boeing 747s to operate these flights. All were painted orange and were generally referred to as 'Big Orange'. One of the carrier's Jumbos, N749WA, is photographed about to turn on to the runway at Miami International in August 1980.

Above: Braniff routes also included South America and McDonnell Douglas DC8s were often used on these services. Photographed at Miami International in August 1980 is N1803E, shown in the same livery as Boeing N471BN but in an alternative colour scheme.

Prior to the revised livery carried by the 727s and DC8s before ceasing operations in 1982, aircraft were to be seen with Braniff International and Flying Colors titles. This photograph illustrates one of the many colour schemes. Boeing 727 N441BN is at New York JFK in August 1978.

One of Braniff's Boeing 727s flew for quite a long time in the livery designed by artist Alexander Calder and N408BN is seen arriving at Dallas/Fort Worth in July 1980.

Above: The airline also engaged Calder to supply a design for one of its McDonnell Douglas DC8s and N1805 was chosen to receive this paint job. The series 62 airliner is being towed at New York JFK on a misty July 1978 morning.

Right: In August of 1978, N1805 was again photographed preparing to depart Miami. Shortly afterwards the aircraft was stripped of paint and re-entered service in the standard Braniff colours.

ALIA — THE ROYAL JORDANIAN AIRLINE

Named after King Hussein's daughter Alia, this carrier is one of several formed by Arab countries since the end of the Second World War. The airline is now known simply as Royal Jordanian. Its current fleet includes Airbus, Boeing and Lockheed airplanes and from its base in Amman, Jordan, passenger and freight services are provided to Middle Eastern cities, together with Europe and the United States.

Above: The carrier adopted a new colour scheme when changing its name to Royal Jordanian at the end of 1986, but photographed before the introduction of the new image is Lockheed L1011 JY AGH. The series 500 is taxying away from its stand at Frankfurt/Main in May 1985.

PEOPLEXPRESS

Peoplexpress was formed in 1981 and quickly built up a fleet of Boeing 727 and 737 aircraft operating low cost services along the Eastern Seaboard of the United States. Initially its fleet consisted of 737s originally flown by the German carrier Lufthansa, and from its base in Newark, New Jersey, Peoplexpress provided high frequency services to various cities including Buffalo, Boston and Baltimore. In 1987, the airline was taken over by Texas Air Corporation and phased into Continental Airlines. At that time People's fleet totalled some 80 aircraft, including eight 747s.

Right: In 1983 Peoplexpress expanded their routes to include Europe and took delivery of Boeing 747s to provide these services. One of the Jumbos taken into the fleet was an ex-Braniff aircraft N602BN which is seen arriving at Newark, New Jersey, after completing a flight from London Gatwick in June 1983.

Overleaf: After the takeover by Continental Airlines, People's aircraft began to receive the titles of the new owner whilst still retaining the original colour scheme. Photographed after new titles had been applied was Boeing 747 N605PE, seen arriving at Newark after completing a flight from San Francisco. After a short stay the aircraft then departed for London Gatwick.

DAN AIR

Dan Air Services Ltd is one of the UK's main charter operators, flying from most British airports to various holiday destinations in Europe. Founded in 1953 by shipping brokers Davis and Newman, the airline was the last carrier to use Comet airliners on regular inclusive tour charter flights. Scheduled services are also provided by Dan Air and its fleet of 50 and more aircraft include examples of Boeing, British Aerospace and Airbus Industry. Dan Air adopted its present colour scheme around 1980.

Built in 1963 and originally flown by Kuwait Airways before coming to Dan Air in 1971, this June 1974 photograph shows the pre-1980 livery of the airline. Comet series 4C G AYVS is seen at Manchester.

Above: Also seen at Manchester on the same day in June 1974, the pre-1980 colour scheme is illustrated on Comet series 4B G BBUV, photographed whilst taxying to the terminal. Prior to becoming a Dan Air plane, this aircraft was in the fleet of BEA.

Right: Undoubtedly a Dan Air Boeing 727 carrying the present livery in use by the airline. G BHVT is a long way from home and is sitting in the heat of the Nevada desert about to leave Las Vegas in April 1985 whilst on winter lease to Minneapolis-based charter airline Sun Country.

NEW YORK AIR

A subsidiary of Texas Air Corporation, New York Air was formed in 1980 offering low cost services from its base at La Guardia, New York to Washington DC with a fleet of McDonnell Douglas DC9s. In the years to follow its routes expanded considerably to include Boston, Detroit and several cities in Florida. The carrier's fleet also increased and before the merger with Continental Airlines in 1987, New York Air's airplanes comprised DC9s, MD82s and the new Boeing 737 series 300.

Below: Photographed in the original New York Air livery at La Guardia airport, New York in June 1983 is DC9 N545NY, with the company's Big Apple logo on its tail.

MUSE AIR

Formed in 1981 by its president, Lamar Muse, this carrier commenced flying between Dallas and Houston, Texas, offering scheduled passenger services with a fleet of McDonnell Douglas DC9s and MD82s. The airline had its base in Dallas and quickly built up services to other North American cities before being bought out by another Texas-based carrier, Southwest Airlines, in 1985. Muse Air DC9s appeared in a totally new livery bearing TRANSTAR titles, but the airline ceased flying towards the end of 1987.

Right: McDonnell Douglas MD82 was photographed at Las Vegas in April 1985 in the original Muse Air livery. This aircraft and all other McDonnell Douglas planes in the fleet were sold to other North American carriers.

FRONTIER AIRLINES

Frontier Airlines dates back some 40 years, having been formed after the acquisition by Monarch Airlines of Denver of three local airlines in the Western States of North America. With its base in Denver, Frontier became one of the major North American carriers, offering flights to over 80 destinations in the United States. During 1986, the airline merged with Continental Airlines and its fleet was taken into their stock.

Frontier had a fleet of McDonnell Douglas DC9s and Boeing 737s, and seen at Albuquerque, New Mexico, in August 1985 is one of their 737s, N7348F.

SOUTHERN AIRWAYS

Southern Airways of Atlanta, Georgia, was formed in 1949 and provided services within the Southern States of the US. In 1979, the airline merged with another North American carrier — North Central Airlines — to form Republic Airlines.

Below: Photographed in the year of the merger, McDonnell Douglas DC9 N92S was one of over 40 aircraft in the fleet. This August 1979 picture illustrates Southern's very simple livery.

NORTH CENTRAL AIRLINES

Formed in 1944, this carrier latterly had its base in Minneapolis-St. Paul. In the summer of 1979, North Central merged with Southern Airways and together formed the new airline Republic. At the time of the merger, the company had a fleet of 60 aircraft including McDonnell Douglas DC9s and Convair 580s, serving almost 90 North American cities.

Right: McDonnell Douglas DC9 N940N in full North Central colours is seen at La Guardia airport, New York, in July 1979. It is from this airport that the airline also operated International flights to Canada.

REPUBLIC AIRLINES

Republic Airlines was a company formed purely through the merger of Southern Airways of Atlanta and North Central Airlines of Minneapolis-St. Paul. Hughes Air West of California was also taken into Republic in early 1980 and this made the newly-formed airline one of the largest domestic carriers in the States. Republic now had a fleet of over 150 aircraft providing coast to coast services.

Left: Boeing 727 N712RC, newly delivered to Republic in 1980, was photographed at Tucson, Arizona, in August of that year. The 727 is shown in the full colour scheme of the new airline and this livery was carried until the appearance in 1984 of a new red and grey design. Not all aircraft were repainted in the new modern style, as Republic itself fell victim to take-over by Northwest Airlines in 1987.

Below: Until it was possible to repaint all the airliners of the combined companies, aircraft were to be seen in hybrid liveries, and this picture shows McDonnell Douglas DC9 N4807S still in the colours of Southern but bearing Republic titles.

AER LINGUS

Formed in 1936 by the Irish Government, Aer Lingus is Dublin based and currently operates an all jet fleet of British Aerospace 1-11s and Boeing 737s, which are used on domestic and European routes, together with three Boeing 747s which provide services from Shannon to the USA. Its livery is predominantly green with the Irish Shamrock in white.

Right: During the latter part of 1976, Aer Lingus leased 737s from other carriers and it was possible to see aircraft in hybrid colours. Landing at London Heathrow in August 1976 is EI ASK in the basic colour scheme of United Airlines of North America. Two months after the picture was taken the 737 returned to United.

Below: This June 1974 picture of Boeing 737 EI ASO at Manchester airport illustrates the livery of Aer Lingus aircraft at that time.

Far right: Originally delivered to Aer Lingus in April 1970, Boeing 737 EI ASH was leased out by them during the winter months of 1975/6 to Canadian airline Transair. The aircraft carried the livery of the Canadian company whilst in service, and returned to Dublin in April 1976. Again operating Aer Lingus flights, the 737 is seen on final approach to London Heathrow in October 1976 still in the basic colours of Transair.

AIR MANCHESTER

This short-lived carrier commenced operations in the early part of 1982 and had its base at Manchester. Owned by parent company Sureway Holidays, the airline operated charter flights on their behalf to holiday destinations. Air Manchester ceased operations towards the end of 1982 when the holding company went into liquidation.

BAC 1-11 G SURE was one of two 1-11s in the airline's fleet, and was photographed about to depart from Manchester in May 1982.

HUGHES AIR WEST

Originally known as Air West, this airline was based in San Francisco and provided scheduled services to cities in the Western States of the USA and Mexico. The carrier commenced operations in 1968 and was renamed Hughes Air West in 1970 when the late Howard Hughes took over control. McDonnell Douglas DC9s and Boeing 727s operated the company's services and before being taken over by Republic Airlines in 1980 had a fleet of over 50 aircraft.

Boeing 727 N722RW was delivered new to Hughes Air West in November 1976 and was photographed whilst turning on to the main runway at Las Vegas in August 1981, almost a year after being taken over by Republic Airlines and still wearing the basic Hughes Air West colours. The 727 went on to fly for Republic and then passed on to serve with Northwest Airlines.

Overleaf: Californians referred to Hughes Air West McDonnell Douglas DC9s as 'Yellow Bananas'. One of the company's DC9s, N9339, is photographed about to leave Los Angeles International airport in August 1977.

AIR CHARTER INTERNATIONAL

This French airline is now known as Air Charter and was formed in 1966 to operate charter services for Air France, its parent company. It has an all jet fleet of Boeing 727, Boeing 737 and Airbus A300 aircraft operating out of its base at Paris-Orly. When the necessity arises the company often leases aircraft from other carriers, including Air France, Air Inter and TAT.

Far left: Air Charter International Caravelle F BJTU at Corfu in August 1983. Built in 1964, the aircraft was delivered to Finnair and flew with the national flag carrier of Finland until becoming a French registered aircraft in 1981.

Left: Caravelle series 3 F BHRK was photographed about to leave London Heathrow in April 1980. Originally delivered to Air France in 1960, the Caravelle had been leased to Air Charter International for a few summer months in 1979. This subsidiary of Air France was formed in 1966 to operate the parent company's charter and inclusive tour services, and whilst operating an Air France scheduled flight the aircraft still carried the logo of the charter company on its tail. The Caravelle was taken out of service a few weeks after the picture was taken and was eventually broken up at the end of 1980.

Bottom left: Whilst operating a charter flight from France, Boeing 727 F BPJU was photographed on approach to Athens airport in April 1977.

TAT (Touraine Air Transport)

Based in Tours, France, TAT originally operated a fleet of small aircraft throughout France. The airline has considerably enlarged its fleet to include Fokker F28 and BAC 1-11 jets, and whilst still known as TAT its meaning has been changed to Transport Aerien Transregional. The airline's fleet now numbers approximately 60 aircraft and its Fokker Fellowship F28s can be seen operating on lease in the colours of Air France. The company also often leases out aircraft to other airlines in other parts of the world.

Below: The Fokker Fellowship F27 is no longer flying with TAT, but in June 1976 one of the company's planes was photographed at London Heathrow in the colour scheme carried by the airline at that time. F BUFA remained in TAT service until 1980.

AVIATECA

Aviateca Guatemala is a Central American scheduled carrier formed by the country's government in 1945. From its base in Guatemala City, flights are made to Mexico and mainland USA. The airline's present fleet consists of three Boeing 737 series 300 aircraft.

Left: Operating a flight from Guatemala City to mainland USA in July 1978 was BAC 1-11 TG AVA, photographed at New Orleans in the colour scheme in use at that time. Aviateca discontinued flying the 1-11 during the early part of 1980, and this airplane was replaced by the Boeing 727 until the 737 appeared in service with Aviateca at the end of the 1980s.

UNITED AIRLINES

United is one of North America's major airlines with a fleet of over 450 aircraft. It is the largest outside the Soviet Union and its routes cover the USA, Canada, the Far East and Japan. Founded in 1931, the airline operates both McDonnell Douglas and Boeing aircraft.

Below: Boeing 747 N4727U photographed at Los Angeles airport in August 1977 was delivered to United in 1973 and is one of eighteen series 122 Jumbos flown by the carrier. The 747 is shown in the colour scheme in use prior to the one currently carried by the company's planes, which was introduced three years earlier.

DORADO WINGS

Based in the Caribbean island Puerto Rico, Dorado Wings operated commuter services in and around the Virgin Islands. The company had a fleet of around sixteen aircraft which performed island hopping duties. In 1982, Dorado Wings was renamed Crown Air and the airline continued to operate under this name before ceasing operations in March 1989.

Handley Page HP137 N4770 was in the fleet of Dorado Wings when photographed at San Juan airport in August 1980.

Whilst operating a passenger charter, Boeing 707 OE INA was photographed as it was being pushed back from the gate at New York JFK in July 1980 en route to Vienna.

MONTANA

This Austrian airline was formed in Vienna in 1976 and its three Boeing 707s provided passenger charters to the USA and the Far East. After a short time in business, Montana ceased flying in 1981.

INTERFLUG

The official state airline of the German Democratic Republic is Interflug, operating out of East Berlin. Its fleet originally consisted entirely of Tupolev and Ilyushin aircraft but in 1989 the airline took delivery of three Airbus A310s which were used to operate scheduled services from Berlin to Havana and the Far East.

Below: Photographed at Amsterdam Schiphol in August 1970 was Tu134 DM SCM. The picture illustrates Interflug's livery of the early 70s which was later discontinued. In early 1981 Interflug replaced the registration letters DM with the letters DDR.

AIR SPAIN

This carrier was based at Palma, Majorca and had a fleet of McDonnell Douglas DC8 series 21 aircraft previously flown by North American airline Eastern. Air Spain provided charter services within Europe and its Spanish island base but ceased operations in 1975, its aircraft returning to Eastern and other American carriers.

Right: Illustrated is DC8 EC CDA in the very attractive Air Spain livery, being prepared to accept a complement of holidaymakers at Manchester airport in May 1974.

WARDAIR

Wardair, the Canadian carrier, used to be purely a charter airline formed in 1952 by Maxwell W. Ward. It was not until 1962 that Wardair commenced operating Transatlantic charters and Boeing 707s were added to the fleet to perform these duties. Boeing 747 and McDonnell Douglas DC10 wide body jets were introduced at a later date, replacing the 707s, and these continued in service with the airline until the autumn of 1989 when Wardair became integrated into Canadian Airlines International.

Right and far right: Boeing 707 C FZYP was photographed at Manchester in August 1975 whilst being prepared to operate a charter flight to Canada.

ONTARIO WORLDAIR

Established in 1978, Ontario Worldair flew inclusive tours from its home base in Toronto to destinations in Europe, South America and the Caribbean. The carrier had two Boeing 707s in its fleet, which remained in service until the company went out of business at the end of 1980.

Below: Previously flown by the Australian airline Qantas, Boeing 707 C GRYN was photographed arriving at Manchester after completing a flight from Canada in the spring of 1979. After the closure of the airline, the 707 illustrated went on to fly for the Royal Australian Air Force.

AIR NATIONAL

Air National, a California based carrier, provided charter flights from the east coast of the USA to London, the Middle East and Greece. Air Canada leased the company one of two Boeing 747s operated by the airline on their North Atlantic flights which, although only in service for a period of around six months, was painted in the colours of Air National. Operations eventually ceased in 1985.

Below: Boeing 747 Combi C GAGA has just attained take-off speed and lifts off runway 31L at New York's John F. Kennedy airport in June 1983.

BRITISH AIRWAYS

The British flag carrier and one of the world's leading airlines. Its routes are world-wide and the airline employ a staff of over 50,000. Formed in 1972 upon the mergers of BOAC (British Overseas Airways Corporation), and BEA (British European Airways), the airline also took over the aircraft and routes of British Caledonian in the early part of 1988 and its European and International routes now depart from both Heathrow and Gatwick London airports.

Right: British Airways Cargo Vickers Vanguard Merchantman G APEG at London Heathrow in the very dry summer of 1976. The Vanguard was delivered to what was then BEA in 1961 as a short/medium haul airliner with seating for around 135 passengers. This particular aircraft was converted into a freighter in 1971 and continued in British Airways service until 1979, before being leased out to other British freight carriers.

Although British Airways was formed in 1972, it was still possible in July 1974 to observe aircraft carrying the original BOAC colours. This photograph shows Boeing 707 G AVPB making its way to the terminal at Manchester. This 707 remained in service with British Airways until 1981, when it was transferred to British Airtours, the charter division of the national flag carrier.

Twelve months later, in July 1975, and 707 G AVPB is photographed again after receiving new titles.

G AWNL, a Boeing 747 series 136 delivered
to BOAC in 1972, photographed at London
Heathrow airport in April 1975 still in the
colour scheme of British Overseas Airways
Corporation.

Below: Boeing 707 G APFB became part of the BOAC fleet in 1960 and continued flying for the airline, later becoming a British Airways aircraft, until the early part of 1975. This 707 was also then transferred to the charter division of British Airways and retitled 'British Airtours'. Photographed at Manchester in July 1975 upon the completion of a flight from the Mediterranean islands, the Boeing was seen in a colour scheme which was not common to the airline.

Bottom: British Airways, like so many other carriers, found it necessary to lease aircraft from other companies during peak periods, and Boeing 737 G BMOR at Manchester in July 1983 is seen in the livery of Air Europe. The 737 is part of a fleet of Boeings operated by Air Europe, a British based holiday and scheduled airline.

PSA (Pacific Southwest Airlines)

North American west coast carrier PSA had their base in San Diego, Southern California, and was regarded as a major regional airline operating services within California, Nevada and Arizona with an all jet fleet. At one time the carrier had more than thirty Boeing 727s in its fleet, but these were later replaced by McDonnell Douglas aircraft, and BAE 146s. In the spring of 1988, PSA was merged into US Air and its fleet eventually repainted in the livery of US Air.

Below: Another variation of livery shown on British Airtours Boeing 707 G APFD, photographed at Manchester in August 1977. This aircraft also flew for BOAC, having been delivered in 1960 and passed to the charter division in 1973.

Right: Boeing 727 N542PS with the familiar smiling face which was to be seen on all PSA planes, was photographed at Los Angeles airport in August 1977.

EFS BAHAMAS

A Nassau based cargo carrier which leased aircraft to operate its freight services. Aircraft were leased to the company by North American Seaboard World Airlines, a major cargo carrier which was later taken over by Flying Tiger Line. Flying Tigers has also been taken over, and its aircraft are flying in the colours of Federal Express, the North American parcels and freight carrier.

McDonnell Douglas DC8 series 61 N8788R was photographed at Athens in April 1977 in the colours of the Nassau based airline.

AIR JAMAICA

Based in Kingston, Jamaica, Air Jamaica currently has an all jet fleet of Boeing 727s and Airbus A300s. At one time, the airline had several McDonnell Douglas DC8s in its fleet which operated flights from Montego Bay and Kingston to London and Frankfurt. Air Jamaica no longer fly to Europe and when these routes were suspended its DC8s were sold. The airline's routes are now confined to the Caribbean, North America and Canada.

Whilst still operating DC8s, Air Jamaica leased this DC8 6Y JGD from South American airline Aero Peru, and the series 51 aircraft was photographed about to turn on to the runway at Miami International in April 1980.

ORION

Orion Airways was a British, Midlands-based tour operator based at East Midlands airport. Services commenced in 1980 with a fleet of Boeing 737s and services were provided from a variety of British airports to holiday destinations in Europe, Spain and the Mediterranean. The airline no longer operates, having been integrated into Britannia Airways, another British-based charter airline, in 1989.

Below: Whilst being instantly recognisable as Monarch Airlines, the British charter airline based at Luton, closer inspection however reveals that this Boeing 737 is carrying the titles and logo of Orion, to whom it was on lease for the summer period. G GPAB was photographed departing the island of Ibiza in August 1984.

COURT LINE

Court Line, one of the first British inclusive tours and charter flight operators to cease operations, was based at Luton. Its fleet consisted mainly of BAC 1-11s, although for a short period two Lockheed L1011 aircraft were also used to provide flights from several British airports to various holiday destinations. Its 1-11s were to be seen in various colour combinations. Upon the collapse of the airline, the 1-11s and L1011s went on to fly with other airlines.

Right: Photographed at Reus airport, Spain, a few months before the collapse of the airline, BAC 1-11 G AXMF is seen operating a flight for holidaymakers from the United Kingdom.

AMBASSADAIR

A travel club based in Indianapolis, Indiana, and at one time having three Boeing aircraft. The club ceased trading in the early part of 1981 and the aircraft were sold to be used by other North American tour clubs.

The airline took delivery of Boeing 720 N8711E 'Miss Indy' during the summer of 1974 and it was used to transport travel club members to various destinations throughout the world. In August 1975, the 720 visited Nairobi, Kenya, and it is there that 'Miss Indy' was photographed.

'SPIRITS HAVING FLOWN'

Not the name of an airline but in fact the title of an album by the pop group The Bee Gees.

Originally owned by American carrier United Airlines, Boeing 720 N7224U continued flying with the airline for thirteen years before commencing a period of leasing. For the singers' 1979 tour the airliner appeared in the colour scheme illustrated, and is seen parked at Miami when photographed in August 1979.

PRINAIR

Founded in 1964, Prinair was based at San Juan International airport, Puerto Rico. Originally known as Ponce Air, the carrier operated extensive commuter services linking Puerto Rico with points in the US and British Virgin Islands, Guadeloupe, the Dominican Republic and other islands within the Caribbean. Services to other destinations on the island of Puerto Rico were also provided. Prinair had the distinction of being the world's largest operator of Herons which were all painted in a standard design in a variety of colours. The airline ceased operations in 1985.

Below: de Havilland DH114 Riley Heron N568PR was photographed on the tarmac at San Juan International airport in July 1978 whilst resting between duties.

ALIDAIR

Originally based at East Midlands airport, Alidair was formed in 1972 as a British leasing and charter operator. Some of the Viscounts in the airline's fleet had the added inscription 'SCOTLAND' on the fuselage indicating that they were under contract for oil exploration in the North Sea operating out of Aberdeen airport. In 1982, Alidair changed its name to Inter City Airlines and continued to operate as previously until ceasing operations in August 1983.

Right: Alidair Viscount G AVIW was photographed whilst parked at Manchester airport in June 1974.

AIR TUNGARU

Air Tungaru was formed in 1977 and is based in Tarawa, situated on one of the Gilbert Islands in the Pacific Ocean. The airline currently has a fleet of three propeller-driven aircraft and its scheduled services from Tarawa to Honolulu are now discontinued.

Boeing 727 T3 ATB, bearing the colours and markings of Air Tungaru, was obtained in 1981 to operate the company's services to Honolulu. The Boeing is photographed about to depart Honolulu in April 1982 and upon the cessation of this service the aircraft returned to North American airline Evergreen.

AIR NIAGARA

Commencing operations in 1982 from its base at Niagara International airport, Air Niagara provided scheduled services from Niagara Falls to Newark, New Jersey. The carrier had two Boeing 727s in its fleet, both series 25 airplanes which were obtained from North American airline Eastern. Upon the collapse of Air Niagara in the summer of 1983, both 727s returned to Eastern.

Photographed at Niagara in June 1982 was Air Niagara 727 N8101N in the full livery of the airline. This 727 was the first one built by Boeing and first flew in August 1963.

SIMBAIR

Simbair, formed in 1971, was a subsidiary of East African Airways with its base in Nairobi, Kenya. Its one Boeing 707 was used to operate charter flights. Following the collapse of the parent company in 1977, Simbair flights were also discontinued.

Below: Photographed at Nairobi airport in August 1975, the airline's one and only Boeing 707, 5X UWM, is seen whilst unloading its freight.

EMPIRE AIRLINES

Empire Airlines was a New York State based commuter airline which began providing services in 1975. Originally, the airline used only propeller-driven aircraft and it was not until 1980 that jet aircraft were to be seen in the company's colours. Empire Airlines disappeared in the spring of 1986 when becoming integrated into the North Carolina based scheduled carrier Piedmont Airlines.

Right: In June 1983, Fokker F28 series 4000 N107UR was photographed as it approached its allocated stand at New York JFK. This aircraft was repainted in the colours of Piedmont and went on to fly with this company.

TRANS INTERNATIONAL AIRLINES

Trans International Airlines dates back to 1948, being formed as a California based charter airline. The carrier had a large fleet of aircraft, including Lockheed Hercules and Electras, and McDonnell Douglas DC10s. Extensive world-wide passenger and cargo services were provided from its Oakland base. In 1979 Trans International became known as Transamerica and, whilst its aircraft retained the same basic livery including the distinctive 'T' logo, new titles were added. Transamerica ceased operations in 1986.

Below: McDonnell Douglas DC8 N8955U, photographed at Los Angeles International airport in August 1977 illustrates the Trans International livery carried by the company's airplanes.

Right: After becoming known as Transamerica, the company's fleet increased with the addition of three Boeing 747 Combi aircraft. Photographed whilst arriving at Manchester in June 1980, N742TV, named 'Uncle Sam', displays the new Transamerica titles. All three 747s continued in service with the airline until 1986, when they were converted into pure freighters and entered service with Cargolux, the Luxembourg airline.

LAKER AIRWAYS

Laker Airways commenced operations in 1966 and provided charter flights and inclusive tours using two Bristol Britannias. By 1978, when the airline started the famous walk-on scheduled transatlantic flights, the now all jet fleet had increased dramatically and included BAC 1-11s, Boeing 707s and McDonnell Douglas DC10s, initially the series 10 and later the longer range model series 30. Laker Airways ceased operations amidst considerable publicity in February 1982.

Below: In 1981 Laker Airways received the Airbus A300s, which were to be used on charter flights to European destinations. The airline received three of these aircraft and the photograph shows the second example to be delivered — G BIMB — about to depart Manchester in July 1981.

Right: 'Skytrain', as the walk-on service was called, initially operated from London Gatwick to New York JFK, and such was the success of the service a further route was added from Gatwick to Los Angeles. The company's DC10s flew these services, and G GSKY, a series 10 version, was photographed about to depart to Gatwick from New York in August 1979.

ITAVIA

Rome based Itavia started operations in 1958 and as Italy's second domestic airline provided scheduled services within the mainland, together with the islands of Sicily and Sardinia. The carrier also ran charter operations with its small fleet of Fokker F28s and McDonnell Douglas DC9s. Towards the end of 1980 the airline discontinued all services.

Whilst operating a flight from Italy, one of Itavia's DC9s, I TIGA, was photographed at Frankfurt/Main in July 1976.

AIR BELGIUM

Belgian charter company Air Belgium International was formed in 1979 and based in Brussels. Originally known as Abelag Airways the country's holiday airline provided passenger charters to European destinations with its fleet of Boeing 737s, configurated to an all economy class layout.

In July 1980, Air Belgium leased 737 OO ABB to operate its summer services and the twin-jet was photographed at Manchester in the livery of Abelag.

PAKISTAN INTERNATIONAL AIRWAYS

PIA — the national airline of Pakistan — began services in 1954 and now operates a comprehensive route system from its base in Karachi.

Below: McDonnell Douglas DC10 AP AXC, photographed at London Heathrow in October 1974, was merely a few months old at the time, and the carrier went on to receive further examples of the class until eventually operating a fleet of four. The illustration shows the old livery of the airline. The DC10s have since been taken out of the airline's fleet, its long haul services now being operated by Boeing 747s.

QUEBECAIR

Based at Montreal, Quebecair was formed in 1952 and operated both scheduled and charter flights. During 1987, the airline became associated with Canadian Airlines International and its titles changed to Inter-Canadian. The airline's title has again been changed, and the company is now known an Intair, this title being applied to the airline's fleet.

Right: At one time, Quebecair had three BAC 1-11s in its fleet, and C FQBR, photographed at Toronto in June 1982, illustrates the original livery of the airline prior to becoming known as Inter-Canadian. All three 1-11s were taken out of service by the carrier in May 1985.

GOLDEN WEST AIRLINES

Southern Californian Golden West Airlines, originally one of the largest commuter airlines in the USA, commenced operations in 1969 flying between Los Angeles and various other California airports. Its fleet consisted of De Havilland and Shorts aircraft, and these types of aircraft remained in service until the airline filed for bankruptcy in 1983.

Below: An August 1981 photograph of one of Golden West's De Havilland Dash 7s seen in the post 1976 colour scheme. N702GW had just arrived at Lake Tahoe airport, California, with an early evening commuter flight from Los Angeles.

Right: One of Golden West's Shorts 330s was photographed at Los Angeles in August 1977 in the pre-1976 livery of the airline.

CP AIR

This Canadian carrier was formed in 1942 as Canadian Pacific, operating out of its base in Vancouver. In 1968 the airline became known as CP Air and operated under this name until 1986 when it reverted to its original title of Canadian Pacific. At that time the carrier's 1968 livery of red, orange and natural metal was replaced with one of midnight blue, cream and red, and this scheme was retained when the title of the airline was later shortened to Canadian.

Left: In June 1974, McDonnell Douglas DC8 CF CPT was operating a summer charter flight from Canada when photographed at Manchester. The airline no longer uses the DC8 and operates its services with McDonnell Douglas DC10s, Boeing 737s and 767s, and Airbus A310s.

ICELANDAIR

Icelandair, the national airline of Iceland, is based in Reykjavic and operates international services to Europe and North America together with domestic services within Iceland. Together with Fokker F27s, the airline's fleet includes Boeing 727s, 737s and 757s, the latter of which are employed on the airline's New York services.

Below: The present livery of Icelandair is basically white with blue cheatline and tail motif, and black ICELANDAIR titles positioned on the fuselage. In October 1976, Boeing 727 TF FIA was photographed whilst visiting London Heathrow on a scheduled flight and is illustrated in the carrier's previous colour scheme.

AFRICAN SAFARI AIRWAYS

African Safari Airways was formed in 1967 with its base in Nairobi to provide flights from European airports to the game parks of Kenya. Its present fleet consists of two McDonnell DC8 series 63 aircraft, and the company's base has been transferred to Basle, Switzerland.

Below: McDonnell Douglas DC8 5Y ASA, photographed at Frankfurt/Main in June 1976, features the distinctive zebra stripes along the top of the fuselage. Whilst the airline retained a similar livery to the one illustrated, the zebra stripes are no longer applied. 5Y ASA is no longer in use, having been broken up in the summer of 1985.

IBERIA

Spain's national carrier Iberia has a large fleet of jet aircraft, basically McDonnell Douglas and Boeing but with a small number of Airbus A300s also. The airline was founded in 1940 and now operates a network of international flights as well as domestic services within Spain and its islands.

Right: McDonnell Douglas DC10 EC CBO, photographed at Las Palmas in April 1976, is wearing the livery of the airline in use prior to the company's current bold yellow and red style.

OCEAN AIRWAYS

A small New Jersey based scheduled commuter airline, originally known as Monmouth Airlines before becoming Ocean Airways in 1979. With its fleet of Pipers, Convair 440s and Beech 99 aircraft, services to destinations in the Eastern States of the USA were provided. Ocean Airways ceased operations around 1981/2.

Below: Martin 404 N147S was photographed at Atlanta, Georgia, in August 1980.

NATIONAL AIRLINES

During the summer of 1980, Pan American took over the Miami, Florida based National Airlines, and all its planes were taken into Pan Am stock. National had a large fleet of Boeing 727s and McDonnell Douglas DC10s, including five long-range series 30s which National used on transatlantic services to London, Paris and Frankfurt.

Right: McDonnell Douglas DC10 series 30 N82NA, photographed whilst working the early evening departure to London Heathrow in May 1980, a few weeks before the take-over. Pan American have since disposed of the DC10s and the aircraft illustrated is currently flying in the colours of American Airlines.

AERO LLOYD

Aero Lloyd, the West German charter airline based at Frankfurt, was established in 1979 with a small fleet of Caravelles obtained from the Spanish airline Aviaco. The carrier later took delivery of McDonnell Douglas DC9s and placed orders for the brand new MD83.

Caravelle series 10R D AAST, one of the aircraft with which Aero Lloyd started business, was photographed in the original livery of the airline at Ibiza in August 1984. Upon delivery of the MD83s a new colour scheme was adopted by the airline.

AEROCONDOR

Aerocondor, Colombia's forgotten airline, provided scheduled passenger and cargo services from its base at Barranquilla, the city in Colombia, Central America. The airline's small fleet included Boeing 707s and 720s together with Lockheed Electras. Aerocondor went out of business in the summer of 1980.

TWA — TRANS WORLD AIRLINES

TWA, one of the North American giants, was founded in 1930 and was one of the first airlines to provide transatlantic flights which commenced in 1946 operated by Lockheed Constellations. The present TWA livery was introduced towards the end of 1974 and is still being carried on the airline's fleet of over 200 aircraft.

Left: Aerocondor provided regular cargo services to Miami, and it is there where Boeing 707 HK1818 was photographed about to touch down in April 1980.

Below: Trans World Airlines' pre-1974 colour scheme is illustrated here, carried on Lockheed L1011 N31008, about to turn on to runway 24L at Los Angeles International in the summer of 1977.

AIR FRET

Established in 1964, Air Fret was a French cargo charter airline based at Nimes-Garons and at the time of closure in the early part of 1980 the company utilized only one aircraft to operate its services.

Originally delivered new to Trans World Airlines in 1959 as a passenger carrying airliner, Boeing 707 F BUZJ was converted into a freighter in 1972. The Boeing was the only aircraft being used by the airline and was photographed at Athens airport in April 1977.

AEROAMERICA

Aeroamerica had a North American base in Seattle and a European base in West Berlin. Formed in 1974, the airline had a large fleet of Boeing 707s and 720s and operated charter flights from its two bases. By early 1980 all of its 707s had been disposed of and flights were provided by the remaining seven 720s, until the airline went out of business around 1981.

Below and overleaf: The two photographs of Aeroamerica's 720s N733T and N734T, both configured into economy class layouts and in different liveries were taken at Las Palmas airport in May 1976.

BRITANNIA AIRWAYS

Britannia is the United Kingdom's largest charter airline, operating an all jet fleet of Boeing 737 and 767 airliners. Its aircraft are to be seen at almost all of the UK airports, carrying holidaymakers to resorts throughout Europe, Spain and West Africa. Britannia 767s are now flying to Australia on charter services. Formed in 1964, its base is at Luton. In the winter months Britannia often leases out its aircraft, whilst in the summer the airline finds it necessary to lease in other 737s and 767s from foreign airlines to enable schedules to be maintained.

Below: On lease to Britannia in August 1987 was 737 G BJBJ, photographed at Ibiza in the colours of Arizona-based America West Airlines.

Right: Also on lease in August 1987 was 737 G BNIA, which was photographed at Ibiza in the livery of Pluna, the South American airline based in Montevideo, Uruguay. This 737 together with G BJBJ operated holiday charter flights from UK airports in the summer of 1987.

Bottom: In May 1982 another Britannia lease shows Boeing 737 G BJZW being pushed back from the gate at Manchester. This aircraft is on loan from Canadian airline Quebecair.

INTERNATIONAL AIR

International Air was a Dominican company formed in 1982 to undertake cargo charter services. Also known as Inair, the airline ceased operations in 1986.

Below: McDonnell Douglas DC8 series 55, originally a freighter in Japan Airline's fleet, made frequent visits to Miami, and it was there that HP950 was photographed in October 1982.

NORDAIR

Formed in 1957 and based at Montreal, Quebec, Nordair provided a network of services within Quebec together with points in North America. Its small fleet of aircraft consisted of Fairchild FH227 and Lockheed Electras, along with ten Boeing 737s. Nordair merged with Canadian Pacific Airlines in 1986.

Right: Photographed in Nordair colours is Boeing 737 C GNDL seen arriving at Toronto in June 1986.

WESTERN AIRLINES

Western Airlines was a long established North American carrier and its history can be traced back as far as 1925. From its base in Los Angeles its large fleet of over 100 Boeing 727s, 737s and McDonnell Douglas DC10s provided scheduled passenger and cargo services throughout most of North America, Mexico and Honolulu. In the spring of 1987 Western merged with Delta Airlines, another North American scheduled airline based in Atlanta, Georgia. The merger created another American giant and the combined airlines now had a fleet in excess of 400 aircraft.

Below: Photographed on final approach to Miami airport in August 1980, McDonnell Douglas DC10 N914WA shows the regular livery in use at the time.

Right: By April 1985, Western had modified their colour scheme and whilst retaining the basic design, the white background to the company's aircraft had given way to the polished fuselage as Boeing 737 N4503W, about to depart Las Vegas, illustrates.

AIR FLORIDA

Commencing services in 1972, Air Florida quickly built up a large fleet of aircraft operating scheduled services within the state of Florida from its base in Miami. Services were later added to include Washington DC and the Caribbean, followed by transatlantic services to Europe flown with McDonnell Douglas DC10 series 30 long-range aircraft. Air Florida had several colour schemes applied to their fleet of Boeings and McDonnell Douglas airliners, and the four pictures here illustrate some of them. In the summer of 1984, the airline went out of business.

Below: One of the McDonnell Douglas DC10s used on services to Europe was N1035F, here photographed in white and blue livery at Miami in May 1980. This aircraft has since been converted into a freighter and flies with Federal Express.

Right: McDonnell Douglas DC9 in Air Florida's orange and blue livery was photographed at Miami in August 1979.

Below: Boeing 737 N40AF is seen in the later blue and green livery.

Right: Towards the end of 1979, Air Florida obtained several Boeing 737s from Singapore Airlines and N46AF, photographed at Miami in May 1980, is seen in the basic livery of its previous owner with Air Florida titles added.

AIR EUROPE

Founded in 1978 as one of Britain's holiday charter airlines, Air Europe now offers scheduled services alongside its charter operations. As with other inclusive tour carriers, the airline often finds it necessary to lease in aircraft during peak periods. Its current fleet is made up of Fokker 100s, Boeing 737s and 757s, and orders have been placed for the new McDonnell Douglas MD11 wide body.

Below: Leased to Air Europe to give extra capacity during the holiday season was Boeing 737 G BJXL. This aircraft was on loan to Air Europe from Air Florida and remained in the livery of the American airline during the duration of its lease. The scene was a very wet June 1983 day at Manchester.

AIRWAYS INTERNATIONAL CYMRU

Welsh airline Airways International Cymru commenced operations from their Cardiff base in 1984, flying charters to holiday destinations. At the time operations ceased in early 1988, the carrier's fleet consisted of two BAC 1-11s and two Boeing 737 jets.

Right: Fully painted in the livery of Airways International Cymru, Boeing 737 G BAZI was photographed about to land at London Gatwick in July 1987. The 737 carries the registration of its previous owner, Britannia Airways.

TAE (Trabajos Aeroes y Enlaces)

This Spanish charter company was based on the island of Palma. Operations commenced in 1967, closed in 1970, restarted in 1973 and closed again in January 1982. The airline's fleet of Caravelles and McDonnell Douglas DC8s were used on inclusive tour flights from Spain to destinations in North Africa and Europe.

Left: McDonnell Douglas DC8 EC CCN was operating a service carrying holidaymakers when photographed at Tenerife airport in April 1975.

TRANSEUROPA

Spanish airline Transeuropa was formed in 1965 and latterly its fleet consisted entirely of Caravelles. From its main base in Palma its fleet was employed providing inclusive tour flights to destinations in most parts of Europe, together with North Africa. The airline ceased operations in 1982.

Bottom left: One of Transeurope's Caravelles, EC BRJ, was visiting the island of Las Palmas when photographed in May 1976.

METRO INTERNATIONAL

A subsidiary of Flying Tigers, the North American cargo carrier, Metro International commenced operating passenger charters in 1981 to destinations which included Europe. Before ceasing operations in 1983, the airline had three Boeing 747s and one McDonnell Douglas DC8 in its fleet.

Below: Metro International leased aircraft from its parent company to operate its services, and Boeing 747 N748TA, seen here in June 1981 at New York JFK, was photographed in the scheme applied to the charter fleet.

SEABOARD WORLD AIRLINES

Seaboard World was a major transatlantic freight carrier, commencing regular scheduled cargo services in the spring of 1956. Based in New York, the airline's fleet eventually included Boeing 747s and McDonnell Douglas DC8s and DC10 freighters, but these aircraft were integrated into the fleet of Flying Tigers when this North American airline took Seaboard World over in late October 1980.

Below: Photographed in April 1980, just a few months before the take-over, was Boeing 747 N704SW in Seaboard World colours about to depart Miami with a flight on behalf of Viasa, the Venezuelan airline.

AEROMARITIME

Originally a subsidiary of French airline UTA, Aeromaritime was formed in 1966 and, from the early part of 1971, operated two Super Guppy aircraft owned by the Airbus consortium carrying parts of the Airbus aircraft between the various manufacturing locations. The airline has since increased its fleet of Super Guppys to four and still operates on behalf of Airbus Industry, although the aircraft carry Airbus Skylink titles. The company is now known as Airbus Inter Transport. Aeromaritime, although still a subsidiary of UTA, now operates passenger services with a fleet of Boeings.

Right: Whilst based at Paris Le Bourget, Super Guppy F BTGV was visiting Manchester in August 1977 carrying out duties on behalf of Airbus Industry. The base of the airline is now located at Toulouse.

SPANTAX

This Spanish charter airline was formed in 1959 and later commenced providing passenger flights from its bases in Palma and Las Palmas. Flights were made to Spain and its islands from various points in Europe until the airline ceased operations in the early part of 1988.

Below: Introduced in 1983, the livery carried by McDonnell Douglas DC10 EC DUG was the last to be applied to any Spantax aircraft and the wide-body was photographed in May 1986 about to turn on to the runway at Palma airport for departure.

Right: In 1976, Spantax was one of the airlines still flying the Convair Coronado 990, of which the carrier had no less than twelve, which remained in service with the airline until its demise. One of the 990s, EC CNJ, originally delivered to Swissair in 1961, was seen in May 1976 at Las Palmas in the pre-1983 Spantax livery.

BRITISH CALEDONIAN

British Caledonian was originally based at London Gatwick before being taken over by British Airways in early 1988. The airline had scheduled services together with charter operations which continued to be served by British Airways after the takeover. McDonnell Douglas DC10 series 10 and 30 aircraft were included in the company's fleet, and the series 10 examples were retitled British Caledonian Charter in the early part of the 1980s.

With all economy class seating, McDonnell Douglas DC10 G BJZE was being used on a return charter to London Gatwick when photographed about to turn on to the runway at Ibiza airport in August 1984. This DC10 was later repainted into the colour scheme of Cal Air, the former British Caledonian Airways charter company and has since appeared in the colours of Novair, the new name given to Cal Air International. G BJZE has had several colour schemes, in fact the same aircraft is pictured on page 68 in the colours of Laker Skytrain.

SABENA

Sabena — the Belgian national flag carrier — flies a worldwide and European service from its base in Brussels. The airline was formed in 1923 and whilst slight variations to its colour scheme have been made over the years, the airline still retains the 'S' logo on the tail of its aircraft.

Below: Boeing 707 OO SJM is shown in the carrier's pre-1984 livery and was photographed at Frankfurt/Main airport in August 1974. Sabena no longer flies this type of aircraft and the one illustrated was transferred to subsidiary Sobelair.

CYPRUS AIRWAYS

Founded in 1947, Cyprus Airways operated both passenger and cargo services from its Nicosia base. By 1974 the airline's fleet consisted entirely of Hawker Siddeley Trident aircraft, all of which were either abandoned or destroyed by the Turkish Air Force at Nicosia airport in July 1974. After the conflict with the Turks, Cyprus Airways commenced replacing its fleet, which currently consists of BAC 1-11s and Airbus aircraft.

Bottom: Hawker Siddeley Trident 2 5B DAC was operating a summer holiday charter to Cyprus when photographed at Manchester in June 1974. Originally delivered to British European Airways in 1968, this plane became part of the Cyprus fleet in 1972, and was one example which was abandoned at Nicosia, returning to British Airways in 1977.

CAPITOL INTERNATIONAL AIRLINES

Capitol was a major North American charter operator formed in 1946 with its base in Tennessee. In 1982 the carrier became known as Capitol Air and with its fleet of McDonnell Douglas DC8s and DC10s the airline continued providing extensive services from the USA to several European points. A variety of colour schemes could be seen on the company's airliners and a selection are to be found in the following illustrations. Capitol Air ceased operations in 1984.

Below: DC8 N912CL, a series 61 aircraft, came into the Capitol fleet in May 1975 and in May 1976 it was photographed at Las Palmas whilst bringing holidaymakers to the island.

Right: Photographed at Miami in October 1984, DC8 N923CL, a series 62 machine, came into the Capitol fleet in June 1984.

Below: Another DC8, N8766, also a series 61 aircraft, was photographed whilst on final approach to Miami airport in October 1982.

Right: In 1981, Capitol Air introduced non-stop flights in each direction between Los Angeles and New York, offering fares lower than other carriers on the route. Services were provided by McDonnell Douglas DC10s specially painted in the SkySaver livery and configured into 360 economy class seating. About to leave Los Angeles with the 8.45 a.m. service to New York is N905WA.

ATLANTA SKYLARKS

Atlanta Skylarks was formed in 1966 as a Georgia-based travel club and operated with a single Boeing 720. The airline and club are now known as Independent Air and whilst the 720 is no longer in its fleet, the carrier now operates a fleet of three Boeing 707s.

Below: Photographed in August 1981 when the airline relied on its only Boeing 720, N7228U was seen visiting Reno, Nevada.

QATAR

Right: BAC VC10 G ARVJ was being operated by the Qatar Government when photographed in 1981. The aircraft was originally delivered to BOAC in 1964 and taken into British Airways upon the merger with BEA in 1972 and is seen arriving at its stand at Terminal 3, Heathrow airport, London. Fifty-four of this type of aircraft were built between the years 1962–1970 and the only examples to be seen today are flying in the colours of the Royal Air Force.

LANICA

Formed in 1945, Lanica operated passenger and cargo services from its base in Managua, Nicaragua, to destinations in and around Central America, together with Miami in mainland USA. The airline went out of business in 1981.

Below: The very colourful livery of the Nicaraguan airline Lanica is illustrated on Boeing 727 AN BSQ, about to make an early morning departure from Miami in August 1978.

ECUATORIANA

Ecuatoriana, the national airline of Ecuador, commenced services from its Quito base in 1974 operating both scheduled passenger and freight services. For a number of years the carrier had only Boeing 707 and 720 aircraft in its fleet, which were painted in psychedelic colours. Although no longer applying this colour scheme to its airliners, Ecuatoriana still retains an impressive livery.

Right: Boeing 720 HC BDP photographed on final approach to Miami in August 1978 illustrates the psychedelic livery which was later replaced by the current scheme introduced in the early 1980s. A McDonnell Douglas DC10 obtained by the airline from Swissair in 1983 flew for a while in basic Swissair colours with added Ecuatoriana titles before receiving the newly introduced scheme. Only the DC10 and Boeing 707s now remain in service with the carrier.

EAST AFRICAN AIRWAYS

Based in Nairobi, Kenya, East African Airways operated a fleet of Douglas DC3s, Fokker F27s, McDonnell Douglas DC9s and BAC VC10s before its collapse towards the end of 1976. The government of Kenya formed a new airline in 1977, which now operates under the title Kenya Airways.

East African Airways regularly used BAC VC10s on services between Nairobi and London and 5Y ADA was photographed at Nairobi in August 1975. The airline received five of the British Aircraft Corporation's series 1153 aircraft between the years 1966 and 1970, which continued in service with the carrier until its collapse.

TRADEWINDS AIRWAYS

Formed in 1968, Tradewinds was originally based at London Gatwick and undertook worldwide freight charters with its fleet of Canadair CL44s. The airline relied on this fleet until obtaining two Boeing 707s at the end of 1977, and the CL44s were gradually phased out in favour of the jet freighters. Tradewinds is now based at Stansted airport and its fleet consists of three Boeing 707s.

Tradewinds was still operating CL44s in April 1976 and G AWOV was photographed at Manchester airport carrying the livery of the airline at that time.

BELIZE AIRWAYS

This airline was based in Belize in Central America and provided both passenger and cargo services in and around Central America, the Caribbean and parts of mainland USA with its fleet of Boeing 720s comprising both passenger and freight carrying models. Belize Airways was formed in 1974, commenced operations in 1977 and continued flying until going out of business at the end of 1981.

Left: Boeing 720 VP HCO was one of the airline's passenger-carrying aircraft, photographed whilst taxiing for take-off at Miami in August 1978.

RIO AIRWAYS

Rio Airways was a Texas based commuter airline operating scheduled services within Texas and surrounding states. At one time the airline had a fleet of around two dozen aircraft, but these became gradually reduced until the company closed in early 1987.

Below: Beechcraft N12RA, a series 99A airliner, was one of six of this type of aircraft in service with Rio when photographed at Dallas/Fort Worth in August 1980.

ARISTA INTERNATIONAL AIRLINES

This American company was formed in 1982 and had its base at New York's John F. Kennedy airport, from where it operated flights to destinations in the USA and Europe. Two McDonnell Douglas DC8s were leased to the airline by Scandinavian Airlines and these were returned to Sweden when Arista ceased operations during 1984.

One of two series 62 DC8s leased to Arista, SE DBI, was photographed whilst visiting Rio de Janeiro in April 1983.

BAC 1-11 C6 BDJ was photographed at Miami in August 1978 and illustrates the Bahamasair livery of the late 1970s. The airline now has a modified colour scheme and its services to Miami are flown by Boeing 737s, the BAC 1-11s having been taken out of service by 1984.

BAHAMASAIR

Bahamasair is the national airline of the Bahamas and was founded in 1973. Based in Nassau, the airline provides scheduled services throughout the Bahamas and to points in mainland USA.

CLUB USA INTERNATIONAL

Club USA International was an Indianapolis based travel club which relied on one McDonnell Douglas DC8 to operate its services carrying club members to various destinations. The operation no longer exists, the club having ceased trading in the summer of 1980.

DC8 N1976P was photographed at Orlando, Florida, in April 1980 and the airliner was one of two ex-Overseas National Airways aircraft specially painted to commemorate the 1976 United States bicentenary celebrations.

Constellation series 1049C HI 228 was photographed at the carrier's home base of Santo Domingo in August 1979. This aircraft continued to fly in the ownership of the renamed company until being withdrawn in 1987.

AEROTOURS

This Dominican Republic freight charter airline was based in Santo Domingo and provided cargo services within the Caribbean and Central America. The carrier changed its name to Aerochago Airlines in 1983 and still operates under this name using a Convair 240 and two Lockheed Constellations.

JET 24

Jet 24 International Airways was formed in 1979 and had its base in Miami from where it operated charter and cargo flights. Known as Jet Charter service, the company leased various types of airliners before ceasing operations during 1988.

Left: McDonnell Douglas DC10 series 40 N133JC, here seen carrying additional Air Panama titles had been sub-leased to the airline from October 1984 until May 1985. The DC10 was photographed in October 1984 about to depart Miami. This aircraft has now returned to and is in service with its original owner, Northwest Airlines.

TEXAS INTERNATIONAL AIRLINES

Texas International, with its base in Houston, Texas, merged with the North American airline Continental in 1982. Prior to the merger, Texas International had a fleet of jet aircraft consisting entirely of McDonnell Douglas DC9s which operated services to all major points in Texas along with several other North American cities.

Below: Whilst still in service with Texas International, DC9 series 14 N1055T was photographed at Houston Intercontinental airport in August 1980.

ALLEGHENEY

Established in 1936, Allegheney Airlines was based in Washington DC and operated scheduled commuter services linking more than 100 cities throughout the North Eastern United States and Canada with its large fleet of BAC 1-11s, Boeing 727s and McDonnell Douglas DC9 series 31 aircraft. In 1979 the airline changed its name to US Air and its route network was enlarged to serve additional points in the USA. Currently the airline has an all jet fleet of around 400 aircraft including those taken into stock following the integration of the North American airline Piedmont in early 1989.

Left and below: In August 1978 Allegheney BAC 1-11 N1113J was photographed at New York's La Guardia airport, whilst exactly one year later McDonnell Douglas DC9 N971VJ was photographed at the same location. These two pictures illustrate the alternative colour schemes used by the airline prior to the change of title.

AIR INDIA CARGO

Air India is the country's international flag carrier, operating an extensive scheduled passenger and freight service with its all jet fleet. The airline does not have pure freighters in its own fleet and regularly leases cargo-carrying aircraft from other carriers as required.

McDonnell Douglas DC8 N776FT, a freighter owned by the late American company Flying Tigers, was being leased to Air India Cargo during the early part of 1981 when photographed at Hong Kong in April of that year. This picture illustrates the close proximity of Kowloon to the international airport.

TRANS EUROPEAN AIRWAYS

Belgian Trans European Airways (TEA) commenced providing world-wide charters and inclusive tour flights in 1971 from its base at Brussels National airport. Its present fleet is made up of Boeing 737s and Airbus Industry airliners, all of which are configurated into all economy class seating.

TEA commenced its services with a Boeing 720 airliner, which was later joined by Boeing 707s. Although both of these classes have now been taken out of service, one of the carrier's 707s was observed and photographed at Tenerife in April 1975, and OO TED was bringing holidaymakers from Brussels to the island.

AIR CARIBBEAN

Air Caribbean commenced operations at the end of 1975 from its base at San Juan, Puerto Rico. With a fleet of five Douglas DC3s, passenger services to St Thomas and the US Virgin Islands were provided. A comprehensive scheduled service of over seventy flights per day was offered by the airline before suspending operations during 1980.

Photographed whilst about to depart San Juan International airport in August 1978 was DC3 N4795.

AIR ATLANTA

From its base in Atlanta, Georgia, Air Atlanta started its low cost high quality scheduled flights at the beginning of 1984 with its fleet of four Boeing 727s. The tri-jets were obtained from other North American carriers and were completely refurbished before being placed into service, incorporating less seating to allow for extra passenger comfort. Air Atlanta continued to operate services throughout the Eastern United States before finally suspending operations in early 1987.

Below: Photographed at Miami in October 1984, this Boeing 727 illustrates the livery carried by all Air Atlanta aircraft.

BEST AIRLINES

Best Airlines was a Cincinnati based scheduled carrier which began operations in 1982. Initially flights using DC9s were made between New York State and Florida, to be followed by scheduled flights between the Eastern and mid Western States. Best Airlines' fleet consisted of two McDonnell Douglas DC9s which remained in service until the company ceased operations at the end of 1985.

Right: McDonnell Douglas DC9 N29259 photographed at Buffalo Airport, New York State, in May 1982 a few weeks after the airline commenced services, was the first aircraft flown by the carrier and can easily be recognised as a British Midland plane from whom Best had leased the series 15 for a few months. The aircraft returned to British Midland in 1982 and is still in service with the East Midlands based airline.